Over 100 gross-worthy facts

WARNING! CONTENTS MAY CAUSE PUKING

WARNING!
DO NOT READ UNTIL AT LEAST HALF AN HOUR AFTER EATING

SCHOLASTIC

SYDNEY AUCKLAND NEW YORK TORONTO LONDON MEXICO CITY
NEW DELHI HONG KONG BUENOS AIRES PUERTO RICO

Scholastic Australia Pty Limited
PO Box 579 Gosford NSW 2250
ABN 11 000 614 577
www.scholastic.com.au

Part of the Scholastic Group
Sydney • Auckland • New York • Toronto • London • Mexico City
• New Delhi • Hong Kong • Buenos Aires • Puerto Rico

First published by Scholastic Australia in 2005.
Text and illustrations copyright © DMAG, a joint venture between
Smartypantz Communications Pty Ltd and Australian Geographic, 2005.
Cover and internal design © Scholastic Australia, 2005.
Illustrations by Greg Costaras, Gimix Enterprises.
Internal design by Tammy Shafer.
Cover design by Kevin O'Sullivan, Smartypantz Communications
and Tammy Shafer.

ISBN 1 86504 656 6

Typeset in Formata BQ Regular.

Printed in China by WKT Company Limited.

10 9 8 7 6 5 4   6 7 8 9 / 0

Contents

WARNING WARNIN

may offend!

may offer

WARNING WARNING

may offend! may offend!

may offend!

WARNING! CONTENTS MAY CAUSE PUKING

Dear Reader

WARNING: what you're about to read could make you sick to your stomach. Your eyes might pop out of your head as you fight the overwhelming urge to vomit. Or maybe you can handle the grossness of what you are about to read?

Have you ever wondered what snot is made of? Or why pee is yellow? Or perhaps why worms still live when you cut them in half? If you have, then this is the book for you. If you haven't then you're in for a treat ... he, he, he.

Yes, this book is packed full of gross questions and answers from real kids who wrote into DMAG looking for answers to some really, really, really gross questions. And now you're also about to find them in the pages of this book...

So let's Get Gross!
(If you think you can handle it!)

Dorothy

Editor
DMAG

P.S. Does your mum, dad, teacher or another grown-up think this book is just TOO gross? Then tell them that it's educational (it's true, you'll learn all about biology) and that should sort them out!

5

Disgusting Digestion

mmm...spaghetti...

Why do we have intestines?

Our intestines help us digest food. They are in two sections – called 'large' and 'small'. The small intestine is over 6 metres long, which is about 5 times the height of your body, but it fits in nicely, coiled up like a bowl of cooked spaghetti. It absorbs all the good stuff (such as vitamins and nutrients) from the food we eat, into the blood stream. The large intestine then removes the water from the leftover, undigested food and turns the liquid paste into solid waste (or poo). And from there it's into the toilet!

What does stomach acid do?

Stomach acid helps digest our food. It is such a strong acid (it has a pH between 1 and 2: that's one million times stronger than water, which has a pH of 7) that it starts breaking down, or dissolving, our food. If this acid, which is actually hydrochloric acid, were to touch your skin, it would burn. A thick layer of mucus lines your stomach to stop the acid burning through it. As well as breaking down food, the stomach acid kills some bacteria and activates a chemical in your body, called an enzyme, which digests protein.

Does bubble gum stay in your stomach forever?

So we've all heard that if we swallow bubble or chewing gum it will stay in our stomach for seven years or even forever. But it's not true. Gum is made from sugar, flavouring, colouring, softeners and plastic, rubber or latex (yes the same stuff they make into rubber gloves!). Your stomach can't digest the rubber so it passes right through your system, usually within 12 to 24 hours. And there's no truth to the rumour that you are then able to blow gum-bubbles out your rear-end!

Why do we need spit?

Spit – otherwise known as saliva – is a form of slime. We make it in salivary glands that are hidden our mouth. We need it to help convert our food to a mush so we can swallow it. Saliva also contains a chemical that breaks down starches – like bread – so the body can use it. Plus it contains another chemical, lysozyme, that destroys bacteria. And lastly it lets us taste our food. The chemicals in the food that give it flavour are dissolved in saliva and then picked up by the thousands of taste buds on your tongue. Without saliva we wouldn't be able to eat. It's so important, humans make over a litre of saliva a day – so you could say we're slime monsters!

Why do cats cough up fur-balls?

Cats are very clean animals. So clean that they lick their fur and bodies to rid themselves of dirt and loose hair. When a cat grooms itself the hair passes through something called the gastrointestinal tract and then exits when the cat does its business. But hair can get stuck in the stomach or intestine and larger clumps of hair can build up. This hair can't be digested and can actually create a blockage. So the cat throws it up – well, wouldn't you!

borborygmi!

You can blame air and other gases for this one. Even if you don't eat with your mouth open you're likely to swallow air, which grumbles and growls as it moves along the digestive tract. And your stomach makes other gases as it noisily churns and mashes food, gas and digestive juices. Muscles in our stomach contract to keep this mixture moving through the digestive system. When bubbles of air are trapped along the way they vibrate, and it's these vibrations that we hear as growling or gurgling sounds. There's even a name for it – borborygmi. The word even sounds like a stomach rumbling – don't you think?

What are kidney stones made of?

The kidneys are clever garbage collectors! Each day, your kidneys process about 190 litres of blood to sift out about 1.9 litres of waste and extra water, which you pass as urine. Kidney stones are solid, stone-like lumps that form in the kidneys out of substances in the urine when it becomes too concentrated – usually from not drinking enough water. They can be as small as a grain of sand or as big as golf balls! But don't worry; it's not common for kids to get them.

MAKE YOUR OWN KIDNEY KIT

how long???

How long is a horse's intestine?

Horses have intestines up to 27m long! Wait a minute – what are intestines? How can they be that long? Intestines (you have two – one small, one large) take mushed-up food from your stomach and break it into basic compounds such as glucose for energy. They also extract water and nutrients. Intestines are a bit like a squishy hose coiled up in your gut. If you were to spread your intestines out in a straight line they would be up to 7.6m long. Once the food has been processed in the intestines it ends up as poo, which is excreted from your body.

If I eat watermelon seeds will watermelons grow in my stomach?

Definitely not! Every part of the watermelon is edible, including the rind and the seeds. Actually, in some cultures it's even popular to bake the seeds and then eat them! There are over 1,200 varieties of watermelon grown worldwide in over 96 countries! And it's so yummy and sweet that it's hard to believe it's good for you! Although watermelons are 92 per cent water, they are full of vitamins A and C and are very high in energy, making them a great energy boost!

How does a cat make a hairball?

When a cat is licking its fur it's not only cleaning, it's removing loose hair. The cat's tongue has tiny barbs that pull loose hair from its coat. The cat will digest small quantities of this hair with no problem, but when too much hair is eaten it forms large clumps that make the cat sick. The cat will heave and make strange noises through its nose and throat, almost like a cough or sneeze. Within few minutes, a hairball is born. YUMMO!

yummo!!

How do people get worms?

The worms people have in Australia are generally fairly harmless. The most common one is the tiny threadworm. You get this by swallowing the worm's eggs, which are so small you can't see them. There are two things you can do to prevent getting worms – don't bite your fingernails and wash your hands before all meals. And if you're ever worried about having worms, speak to Mum or Dad. If you have threadworms don't worry. All you need to do is take a tablet and they'll go away. Easy!

Why do cows regurgitate their food?

Cows regurgitate – or spew up and re-swallow – their food in order to digest it. Humans can't digest grass but cows, thanks to their four stomachs and their spewing trick, can. When the grass is swallowed it goes into a chamber (one of the four 'stomachs') where it is mixed with bacteria. Then it moves to another area where the bacteria grows rapidly, feeding on the grass. Hours later, the cow regurgitates the mixture, called cud, chews it for a while, and then swallows it again, diverting it into the third then fourth chambers. All this is so it can break down the proteins and carbohydrates in the grass. But most of what it ends up eating is bacteria.

It's All About Poo

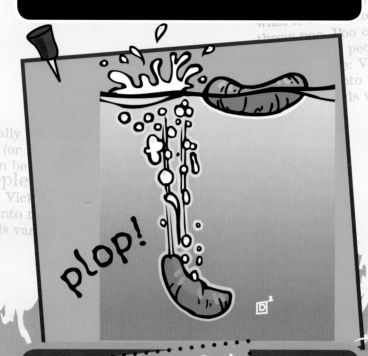

plop!

Why do some poos float and some poos sink?

Believe it or not poo can be a guide to a person's health. Generally, floating poo is a good thing. It means there's enough fibre, water and looseness in your poo to pass through your body easily. If they sink, it means they've been compacted, maybe because there wasn't enough fibre. Fibre is mainly needed to keep the digestive system healthy. It is found in fruits, vegetables, nuts, seeds, dried beans and wholegrain foods.

Why do we get constipated?

So you're having trouble doing a poo. Well, that's constipation! But to understand constipation, it helps to know how the large intestine works. Food flows through the small intestine as a liquid mixture of digestive juices and food. By the time it reaches the large intestine, all the nutrients have been absorbed and the large intestine has one main function: to absorb water from the liquid waste. But sometimes too much water is absorbed, leaving a very hard and dry stool (poo) that can't be passed without straining.

arrghh!!!!

What happens to all the poo, wee and vomit that aeroplanes drop in the sky?

When you flush the toilet in a plane, vacuum pressure sucks it down a tube and into tanks in the cargo hold, under the plane. And there it remains until the plane returns to the ground. It is then slurped out with hoses – ewww! But occasionally planes do drop nasty surprises; nick-named 'blue ice', because the blue toilet disinfectant mixes with the poo which then freezes as it leaves the plane. Chunks of blue ice have been reported in the UK and US recently, although most airlines say the poo is not from them.

splattt!!!

Why do people get diarrhoea?

Diarrhoea, which is when you have runny faeces (faeces is a nice way of saying poo), usually occurs because you've eaten or drunk something that has nasty bacteria in it. It can also occur if you've eaten a food that irritates you or if you're extremely nervous or scared. Your intestines, which normally soak up water from the food you've eaten, actually add water to the poop to make a mush that can quickly be pushed through your body. The idea is to get rid of the bad stuff as soon as possible.

Types of poo

THE TORNADO – A massive storm of poo bottom requires lot's of wiping.

THE CARROT – Poo that has small pieces from last night's dinner.

THE STEAMY LUMPY – A big one, really

PELLETS – Small pieces of poo about the bubblegum ball. Rabbits do these

ol Laying a cable submarine

Dropping a

WARNING WARNI

may off

may offend!

19

FIRE BOMB – Hot ... painful.
Often found after ...
S... ...
that ...es out
wiping the

THE TORN...
from your ...

THE CARR...
carrot in ...

THE STEAM...

PELLETS – S...
size of a bubblegum...

Do snakes poo?

Snakes don't have a bladder, so both poo and wee come out through the same opening, which is found just behind a snake's tail. All waste is stored in the cloaca, and some snakes have glands that also empty into here. These glands contain foul-smelling musk, which can be ejected when the snake is frightened or threatened. The poo, because it is mixed with wee, comes out as a runny light-brown or yellow mix that looks a bit like peanut butter. Think about that next time you're biting into a sandwich!

Everything that's in the toilet when you flush gets washed into sewer pipes. The mix of water, poo, paper and urine – called sewage – eventually ends up at a sewage treatment plant. Here the solids are filtered out and the remaining liquid is treated and released to rivers or the ocean. In some cases the water is treated in such a way that it can be recycled as non-drinking water for use in toilets and gardens. Sometimes the solids – which are renamed biosolids – are used in fertiliser. So some of our poo does end up on the ground – and you were worried about stepping on dog poo!

Why is manure good for plants?

Anybody who has ever had to muck out a stable knows what manure is! It is a mixture of spilled feed, urine (otherwise known as pee), hay and poo from livestock such as cattle and horses. Manure contains the nutrients nitrogen, phosphorus and potassium, which plants really like. When manure is worked into the soil the plants are able to take these nutrients up through their roots. So you could say plants are manure-munchers.

21

1. poo

Poo is brown, usually...
fresh – no one kn...
(or so they say)...
poo. Poo can...
short and...
friends nic...
Vicki-poo...
it can (h...
rapidly f...
depending...

Why does poo stink?

Poo – or if we're going to use the polite word for poo – faeces (fee-cees), smells because of bacteria. We have millions of microscopic bacteria in and around our bodies. There are good and bad kinds of bacteria. The bad kinds make us sick. Some of the good kinds live in our intestines. As they munch through our food they make two chemicals that stink – indole and skatole. So it's normal for poo to smell. But here's a really gross fact – up to half the material we poo is actually bacteria. Yikes!

Why do wombats have square poo?

Now that's a good question. So good, in fact, that even some of the world's greatest scientists can't explain it! The poo is probably shaped this way in the intestines. But why? We know that their roughly cube-shaped scats are used to mark their territory. Usually wombats leave them on high pieces of vegetation and land such as logs, rocks or even a mushroom. So maybe it's square so it doesn't roll away? That would be clever!

How do laxatives work?

Just in case you don't know, laxatives are used to help with constipation! Some laxatives swell up inside your intestines. This makes your stool (poo) grow bigger and softer, which encourages your bowels to move and push the stool out quicker. Other laxatives reduce the amount of water absorbed from your bowel, which increases the amount of water in your stools. The water softens the stool, making it easier to pass.

Why do dung beetles collect poo?

Dung beetles are interested in poo for two main reasons. Eating and nesting. What they don't eat they roll into balls and push underground. Then the female beetle lays her eggs in the ball. When the youngsters hatch they have a ready supply of food. Now before you say 'that's gross!' think what life would be like without the dung beetle. There'd be poo from animals everywhere. In fact up until 1951, cattle farmers in Australia had paddocks covered in dung. Since cows weren't native to Australia, a beetle hadn't evolved here to get rid of their dung. So we had to import the dung beetles. Strange but true!

WARNING WARNIN

may offen

may offend!

Why is poo brown no matter what colour food you eat?

You eat food to give you energy. When you digest food, your body takes out the good stuff that it needs and gets rid of stuff it doesn't. Your body also gets rid of other stuff such as old blood cells. When it processes these cells a chemical called bilirubin is created and it's brown. This chemical gets mixed with your left-over food matter and hey presto – brown poo!

Do fish poo while swimming around in their tanks?

J ust like any creature that eats food, fish need to get rid of toxins from their bodies. Actually fish go to the toilet quite often. Just watch patiently and you're sure to see some long stringy poo emerging! Fish also excrete ammonia (their equivalent of urine) via the gills into the water. Yes! Gills aren't just used for breathing as you may think; they also get rid of wastes! But ammonia is invisible and very toxic to fish – a good reason to clean your tank regularly!

Wee

What does wee smell like?

Fresh wee — or urine — usually doesn't have a strong smell. Some people's urine smells after eating asparagus, and if it smells sweet it can be a sign of diabetes or a very rare condition called maple syrup urine disease. However, while fresh urine usually doesn't smell, old urine does. When it's left for a while, for instance in a nappy, a chemical in it called urea starts breaking down into ammonia and carbon dioxide. And the ammonia — which is also used in cleaning products — smells. If it's really strong it's enough to make your eyes burn. Lovely!

Why does pee change colour?

Pee, wee, or urine – whatever you want to call it – gets its yellow colour from a chemical called bile, which is made by your liver to break up fat in the food you eat. If you drink a lot of water, your pee will be lighter coloured. If you are dehydrated (which means you haven't drunk enough water), your pee will be darker yellow. Only a few foods affect the colour of our pee – and you have to eat a lot of them: beetroot can make it red, rhubarb can make it brown. Quite a few medicines and vitamins also change the colour of pee – if you take riboflavin, a B vitamin, your pee turns bright yellow.

1. pee
Pee or wee is yellow or sometimes clear, just like is usually very warm. I had to describe the sound would be a tinkling. lone in the toilet but som in your pants, near a t in the shower and in the place... POOL it is sme Loud, hard laughter ca sometimes lead to letting a small amount of pee. I be mistaken for juice, nells different.

Why is pee yellow?

It's all thanks to bile, a chemical that breaks up fat in your liver. The bile itself breaks down to urichrome, which is the substance that makes pee yellow. About 95 per cent (that's nearly all) of pee is water. The more liquid you drink the more water there will be and the lighter your pee will be. Pee also contains about two tablespoons worth of urea, a substance that is also found in your saliva, your sweat and even cleaning products – eeeww!

Why is our wee warm?

The normal body temperature of a healthy resting human is 36-37 degrees Celsius. Even a few degrees above can result in death. So you have a very clever body that works hard to keep its insides at a constant temperature. Because your wee is inside your body long before it enters the toilet, it is kept at body temperature, which means it is still very warm as it leaves.

-36°

Do birds wee?

They do and they don't. Unlike most other animals, a bird wees – or urinates – through the same opening that poo – or faeces – comes out of. This means that things can get mixed up a bit. Also, bird droppings have a third component called urates, which is a cream-coloured waste product produced in the kidneys. So the white part of bird droppings is urates, the brown part is faeces and the liquid part is wee.

Pee or wee is yellow or some—— just like Poo it is usually very warm. If you had to describe the sound of pee it would be a tinkling. Pee is done in the toilet but sometimes in your pants near a tree, in the shower and in the main place... POOL it is smelly. Loud, hard laughter can sometimes lead to letting out a small amount of pee. It can be mistaken for ice, but it smells different.

WARNING WARN
may offend!
may o

Ants both poo and wee but it's usually together as light brown droplets, though since they only have little throats and swallow only liquids and very small particles, they don't produce very much. But they do actually 'go to the bathroom'. Ants use out-of-the-way chambers in their nests as bathrooms. They also deposit rubbish in the same chambers. Garbage consists of uneaten prey, empty cocoons and dead ants. But of course when they're outdoors, the ants simply go to the toilet wherever they happen to be.

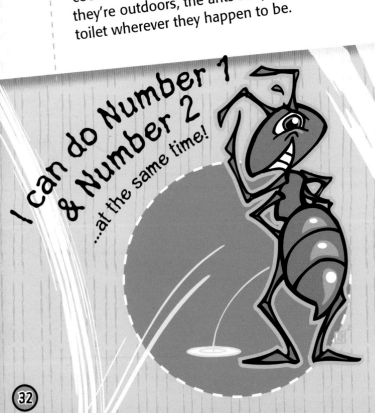

I can do Number 1 & Number 2 ...at the same time!

drink up??

Is it safe to drink urine?

No! Urine is mostly water, but this doesn't mean it qualifies for the recommended 6-8 daily glasses of water. Urine also contains small amounts of hundreds of other things including nitrogen, potassium, sodium and dangerous poisons that must be removed from your body. If you drink it, you're taking these dangerous poisons back in. But what if you're dying of thirst? Ex-SAS (Special Air Services) hero Chris Ryan, who walked 400km through desert in enemy territory, didn't drink his urine even when he ran out of water. 'It can do your body quite a lot of harm,' Chris said.

Snotty Noses
& Goobers

Why is snot green?

Snot isn't just green, it's brown, yellow ... even black if it's filled with coal-dust. Snot's colour comes from two main things, the mucus it is made from and the gunk that it traps – such as smoke, pollen, germs and dirt. Mucus – or slime – is a thick sticky protein, and it's in our nose to trap things so they don't reach our lungs.

What is snot made of?

S not is made from mucus, which is really the same as slime. Now before you go 'eeew gross!' you should know that mucus is very important to us. It's also found in lots of places other than your nose, though in slightly different forms: your mouth (as saliva), throat and stomach to name a few. Mucus stops things drying out (ever had a dry mouth?), lubricates things (it would be hard to swallow without saliva) and acts as a protective barrier. And the last one is the main reason you have it in your nose. The mucus, which is a thick, sticky protein, traps things that we don't want reaching our lungs: such as germs and smoke or dust particles. And here's a really gross fact - we actually swallow about half a litre of snot a day! Yum!

1. **snot**
Fluid from your **nostrils**, known as **mucus** but often called snot. Many people think it's green but it can be all colours. Someone who sneezes a lot could be called a **snot rocket**. Snot can be difficult to manage when you have no tissues or hanky, the most common place to **wipe** snot is on a sleeve. Snot is not to be mistaken with **boogies** which are often found **under desks** at school.

WARNING WARN
may offend! may of

How does snot get in your nose?

Our nose makes snot, otherwise known as mucus, all the time. The snot is there for a reason. It traps germs, dirt and bacteria for you. When you've got a cold, your nose goes into snot-making overdrive to try and stop the germs getting into your lungs. Even when you're healthy your nose makes about one cup of snot a day. So face it – we're all snot machines!

A cup of snot a day!!

Why do people pick their nose then eat the boogers?

Because they like the taste? OK, our nose filters the air we breathe and gets rid of germs when you have a cold. For proper breathing it's necessary to clean your nose – picking it is one option. However, it's your choice to eat them. Apparently some people find boogers quite tasty (salty). Other people eat boogers because they suffer from a mental disorder. In ancient India, some people believed that it led to a better sense of smell and a smooth complexion. It's not a theory I'm keen to test!

Why do we sneeze?

AHHH – CHOO! Don't hold back your sneezes – let 'em rip. If you just sneezed, something (such as dust, cold air, or pepper) was probably irritating or tickling the inside of your nose and sneezing is your body's way of removing the irritation. When the inside of your nose gets a tickle, a message is sent to a special part of your brain called the sneeze centre. The sneeze centre then sends a message to all the muscles that have to work together to create a sneeze and that irritation is sent flying out of your nose. A sneeze is a reflex, which means you do it automatically without thinking, so nope, there's no way of stopping it.

Why do we get nosebleeds?

Get your finger out of there! Did you know nose picking is one of the main reasons kids get nosebleeds? But it's not the only reason. Most nosebleeds start at the front part of the nose in your nostril when the tiny blood vessels that line the inside of your nose are broken by being scraped, ripped or irritated. These blood vessels are very fragile and lie very close to the surface, which makes them easy targets for injury. Some common reasons are sneezing, nose blowing, being hit in the nose and dry, hot air.

, known as
not. M
all co
alled
fficult
hank
not is
boo!
ks a

What is mucus?

It's that slimy, gooey stuff probably better known to you as snot. Your nose makes about a cupful (about 200 millilitres) each day! But it's not just found in your nose. Mucus is made in mucus membranes in all sorts of places: the stomach, intestines, nose, lungs, eyes, mouth, and the urinary tract all contain mucus membranes. And it has a pretty important job – it protects your body from invaders such as germs and dust, helps you swallow and even protects the inside of your stomach from its own acid.

picked a winner!

Why do people produce more snotty mucus when they have a cold?

Call it what you want – snot, mucus, boogers, phlegm or slime – that gross stuff in your nose works hard to keep you healthy. Snot is made to protect the body from invaders such as germs, pollen and dust. The snot traps the tiny particles of junk that you breathe in so they don't make their way into your lungs and make you sick. If germs do sneak in, and you get sick, you'll probably get a runny nose because your body makes extra snot to wash away the germs.

Why do people snore?

Unlike what many people think, snorers actually don't sleep well. They can't get the deep restful sleep they need, because snoring causes them to briefly wake up, even though they don't remember it. Almost everyone snores (actually about one in eight people do, so there's sure to be someone at a sleep-over). Even if you don't snore regularly, chances are you snore now and then. The reason you snore is that while you're asleep the muscles that normally keep your throat open go into relax mode and sag inward. When these muscles become too floppy, they block your airway and you start to snore.

z z z z z

1. **snot**
Fluid from you~~r~~ ~~as~~ ~~a~~ny p~~eo~~ple
mucus but often ~~other~~ colours. ~~s~~omeone
think it's green but it can be ~~different~~
who sneezes a lot could be called a **s~~n~~**
rocket. Snot can be difficult to ~~es or hanky, the~~ ~~Snot~~
wher~~e~~
com~~e~~
is n~~o~~
ofte~~n~~

What is phlegm?

Phlegm is a build up of mucus (snot) that you cough up from the lungs. It's a mass of sticky mucus mixed with pus-like material and dead white blood cells. 'Healthy' phlegm is normally clear or white. Yellow phlegm is normally a sign of infection. But green or brown phlegm probably means a trip to the doctor. Phlegm is released from glands in the walls of the bronchi (airways) and from cells lining the nose and sinuses.

What makes slugs slimy?

The simple answer is it's your old friend snot (or mucus). Slugs ooze a slimy substance whenever they crawl. The slime makes it easier for them to move and protects them. A slug could crawl over an upright razor blade and would not get cut! But what this mucus is made up of is still something of a mystery to scientists. It is very sticky and makes good glue.

WARNING WARNI!
may offend!
may offe

Why do dogs sniff other dogs' behinds?

When humans greet each other they use two of their strongest senses – sight and sound. But a dog's strongest sense is its smell. A dog's nose has about 100 million smell cells whereas humans only have about 10 million. So instead of a dog asking its mate 'how are you?' it is easier for it to sniff the dog's bum and tell straight away. The sense of smell is so powerful it's thought the dog can pick up what the other dog has eaten, whether it's happy and how healthy it is. We wonder if they fart when they say hello? Mmmm...

Why do dogs roll in disgusting things?

Although there are a few theories about this, they all relate back to when dogs were creatures of the wild, that is, wolves. One theory is they rolled in smells to disguise their scent, so that when they were hunting, their prey wouldn't smell a 'dog' coming (they'd just smell something else). Others think they did it to let the rest of the pack know they'd found something interesting. But it could just be that they enjoy it – smell is their strongest sense after all!

Barf-O-Rama

L ots of things: spoiled or bad-tasting food; too much food or drink; poisons; viruses; bacteria; nervousness; extremely disturbing sights, motions such as a rocking boat ... When you vomit, the muscles around your stomach contract, the valve that stops food coming back up the tube leading to your mouth opens and that lovely mixture of stomach acid, mushed-up food and mucus flies out. Yum!

barrff!!!

vomit
There are many ways to say ... the words
...mit or throw up are usually...
...ese are the others: ...
Chuck
...url Spew
Puke
Chunder
Regurgita...
Barf
Up-chuck
Splurge
.Throw up
Hork
Liquid Scre...
Toss a sidew...
Revisit your brea...
Technicolour yaw...
Loo...
Ta...
Gr...
Be...

Why does vomit always have carrot in it no matter what you've eaten?

When you haven't eaten any carrots, it's very weird to find something that looks like carrots in your vomit! And that's why you'll be happy to know it's not carrots! In your diet you have fats, proteins and carbohydrates. In your stomach, the acids act on the fats and make them into little reddish globules. Why they're red we don't know, but it's this fat that looks like carrots. If you're game, you can prove it's not carrot by biting a globule. Eeeew! No, don't!

There are many ways to say vomit, the words spew or throw up are usually the... Here are the others: ...

pyschedelic yawn!!!

Chuck

Spew

...ke

...hurle...

...egurgitate...

...f

...p-chuck (similar...

...plurge

Throw up

...ork

Liquid Scream...

...oss a sidewalk pizza

...Revisit your breakf...

...echnicolou...

...oose your lunch

...ango with...

...reet your...

...Become a multicolou...

Is there anything else in spew other than what you just ate?

Vomit is the mushed-up, half-digested food from your stomach, plus a little slimy stomach mucus, a dash of saliva, some stomach acid and other chemicals that help digest food. The stomach acid in spew can be so strong it will take the paint off your bike. And that lovely green colour comes from a chemical called bile (the chemical you can also blame for the disgusting taste). Bile is made in the liver, stored in the gall bladder and then used in the small intestine, the place your mushed-up food goes after it leaves the stomach. Sometimes some of the mush from your small intestine gets squeezed back up into the stomach and then just keeps going up, up, up – spewing!

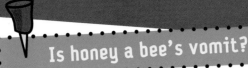

Is honey a bee's vomit?

Yep it is – well sort of! The bees that collect nectar from flowers have two stomachs – one for food and one to store the nectar in to take back to the hive. At the hive, this forager bee vomits it up and passes it on to another bee that rolls it around in its mouth before putting it into a cell made of wax. Over time the nectar condenses and becomes honey. See – not all spew is bad!

How does vomit get from your stomach to your throat?

Vomit – that lovely mix of food, spit, stomach acid and snot (yes that's right – snot!) – leaves your stomach because the brain tells your intestines to start contracting. This squeezes the food up your oesophagus (oh-sof-a-gus) into your throat. Along the way a valve that sits between your stomach and the oesophagus, opens to let the food out. Thankfully it all happens very quickly!

ow up are usually the most acceptable. These are the
others: To **vomit** is to:
Chuck
Hurl
Spew
Puke
Chun
Regur
rf
Up-chu
plur
Throw
rk
Liquid
ss a
Rev
chnic
se you
ngo
t your
me a

How do flies eat?

The hairs on a fly's feet are used for tasting! If they walk on something yummy (which for a fly is anything and everything) they then taste it with their mouths. But before eating it they spit and vomit on it. Flies like their food to be liquid so they can suck up their food like we drink using a straw. Their saliva liquefies the food. Flies also often go to the toilet while eating. Think about that next time a fly lands on your sandwich – gross!

lunchtime!

urge Throw up
. Liquid Scream
s a sidewalk pizza Revisit your breakfast
chnicolour yawn Loose your lunch
ngo with the Toilet Greet your guts

Why do dogs eat grass then spew it up?

This age-old question has never been resolved. Do dogs know that if they eat grass they'll spew? Dogs are mainly carnivores (meat-eaters) but don't mind a few vegies. It's possible they're eating the grass to get the extra vitamins. Unfortunately, not all grass agrees with them. But some people think they eat the grass because they already feel crook and want to spew. There's no denying they're sick after they eat the grass but are they sick before they eat it?

Gross Gas

Why do people fart?

Farts are caused by gas – some of it smelly – escaping out your rear end. Most of this gas is produced in the intestines (see the question on page 6 to find out what the intestines do), but some of it is swallowed when you eat your food. Some gas escapes out your mouth before it reaches your intestines. This is, of course, burping. The average human burps or farts between ten to 15 times a day, although we're not always aware of it.

To break wind, pass gas, fluff or flatulent are polite ways to express the motion. It can also be known as:

Popping off
Blasting the butt trumpet

Why do some farts smell and others just make a loud noise?

$$x + y = z$$
speed + butt muscle = sound

As you've obviously noticed, all farts are different. The sound is produced by vibrations in the ... let's call it the bottom hole, but its real name is the anus. The loudness or softness depends on the speed that the fart leaves your bottom and the tightness of your muscles in that area. The odour comes from small amounts of hydrogen sulfide gas and skatole in the mixture. The more sulfur-rich your diet the more your farts will stink!

What a ripper!!!

Why do beans make us fart?

The gaseous after-effects of baked beans aren't exactly the fault of the humble legume – bacteria in your large intestine do the dirty work. Beans contain sugars that we humans cannot digest. When these sugars reach our intestines they still contain valuable nutrients, so the bacteria go wild and have a big feast. As they gulp down the big sugars, they let out lots of gas! But believe it or not bean farts don't usually smell! Other famous fart-producing foods include corn, capsicums, cabbage, milk, and raisins.

Why do some farts stink and others don't?

Farts are caused by gases made in the large intestine. Bacteria in the intestines ferment undigested food. During this process, gases such as hydrogen sulphide, otherwise known as rotten-egg gas, are made. Some foods, especially ones high in complex carbohydrates, such as beans, tend to make more gas because starch easily ferments. And the more rotten egg gas the smellier your fart is!

...s include:

A Ripper – A really big one, loud a

Silent but Deadly – Vile

...p on you after it is released from the
...butt, suddenly hits you with deadly f

Whiffer – Can be smelt m
one can be sure where it cam

– The stinkie
a thre

WARNING WARNI
may offend! may off

I. gas

Often **silent but deadly**, sometimes loud and proud – fart ᏀᎯᏚ share's the common characteristic of being INVISIBLE and GROSS! Farts are often occur when you eat too many **tacos or beans**. They emit straight from your bottom and out into the world to say a **foul HELLO**. When it's your own fart it's bearable, but when it's someone else's it can be woeful. Celebrities **fart** just as much as anyone, think of a celebrity that you think is really good looking...he or she farts about 14 times a day. If you sit on a **metal chair** and fart it can amplify the sound. Farts lie dormant in your **rectum** until you let em rip.

WARNING WARNI
may offend!
may

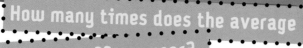

It is really hard to count how many farts a person does in a day, because people fart the most when they are asleep. But on average, a person produces about half a litre of fart gas per day, which equals about 14 daily farts. If you multiply that by 365 days, that's 5110 farts per year. So let's say you live to be 83, that's 424,130 farts in a lifetime! Actually it's more than that, because people even fart after they die!

5 down, 9 to go ...

Skin, Scabs & Pus

Why do teenagers get pimples?

It's your sebaceous glands spewing sebum! What? A tiny collection of cells lie just underneath your skin at the root of the millions of nearly invisible hairs that grow all over your body. Normally they produce small amounts of a waxy, oily substance called sebum that seeps out of the holes or pores in your skin. But when your body starts to change into an adult's, you make chemicals called hormones that make your sebaceous glands work overtime. They go a little crazy, oozing way too much oil, which plugs up your pores. Bacteria feast on the oil, multiply and cause areas close by to become red, swollen and ooze pus – a pimple is born.

Why and how do we get blisters?

Blisters are the body's way of protecting itself. When the outer layer of skin is repeatedly rubbed and irritated, the skin creates its own version of bubble wrap to protect the deeper tissue. The watery part of blood, called serum, oozes into the loosened gap between the second and the top layers of skin. The fluid fills the space, creating a water-filled pillow of protection.

so gross!

ifferent kinds of
ad zits:

ANO – ready to
ving pus all

SE – a really, really

izza – A colony
p together creating
t, complete with
y zit-cheese.

What are fingernails made of?

Nails are made of keratin, the same tough, fibrous protein that is found in eagle talons and rhino horns and also in your own hair and skin. Even though it may look as if your fingernails and toenails start growing just where you can see them, there is actually all kinds of nail stuff going on behind the scenes! Nails start in the nail bed, a flat surface that is under your nails and starts about 7mm beyond where you can see. When cells at the root of the nail bed begin to grow together to form keratin, a nail is born! As new cells grow, older cells become hard and compacted and are eventually pushed out toward your fingertips.

another mystery solved!

smooch!

Can you really get warts from frogs?

No (same as you can't get princes)! The human papilloma virus (HPV) causes warts and can be passed from person to person. But you can't get it from kissing frogs (or toads). The myth probably started because many toads have bumps on their skin that look like warts. But that doesn't mean you should go around kissing them! Toads do secrete a substance from the skin that can be very irritating if it comes in contact with your eyes, nose and mouth. The large bumps behind a toad's ears contain a nasty poison, which can even cause death to predators. So watch out!

What's a scab?

Scabs are made from the blood, which contains many types of cells that are so tiny they can only be seen with a microscope. Platelets are one type of cell. They rush to the site of a cut and stick together – clot – so that more blood doesn't come out and germs don't go in. As the clot dries it forms a crusty, red-brown scab. Under the scab your skin starts healing. We know it's tempting but don't pick your scabs – it will take them longer to heal!

What is pus?

Pus is a whitish-yellow liquid that forms when you have an infection. It's made from dead germs, like bacteria, and even some of your body's good white blood cells that died while gobbling up the germs. Sometimes so much pus is formed that it will cause the infected area to swell. Over time your body will drain off the pus. When the infection is near the surface, as with a pimple, some people prefer to squeeze the pus out – gross! While it may feel better, it can sometimes make the infection worse.

Why does our hair fall out?

Most people lose about 50 to 100 hairs every day – and it's a good thing, because we'd all look like huge hair-balls if we didn't! The hairs grow from follicles, which are very tiny holes deep in your skin. Each follicle contains a hair root, the part of the hair that is alive and growing. But the part of the hair that you love, wash and brush is actually all dead. About 85 out of 100 hairs on your head are growing at any time.

Why does our skin peel?

Our skin is continually being renewed – the very top layer of our skin, the stratum corneum, is made of dead, flat skin cells that constantly shed everywhere. In one minute we shed 30,000 to 40,000 microscopic skin cells from our body. That's about 4kg of dead skin per year! Peeling after sunburn is your body's way of getting rid of damaged cells. Cells damaged by the sun are at risk of becoming cancerous, so all damaged cells are instructed to die, resulting in whole layers of damaged skin peeling off, to be replaced by other cells underneath those layers.

How much skin do we shed each day?

Every minute we shed about 35,000 microscopic skin cells – in a day that adds up to about 11grams of skin and in a year that adds up to a massive 4kg. In fact the dust in your home is mainly made up of your dead skin, which makes a tasty treat for dust mites. Yum!

Skin - the stuff that hold
making sure your body do
Has no flavour.
Scabs - something
appea
Somet
scab
P
liq
wh

Why do we get moles on our skin?

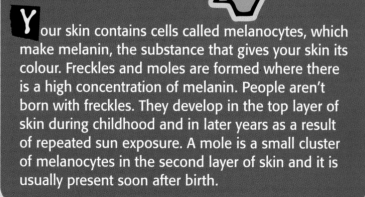

Your skin contains cells called melanocytes, which make melanin, the substance that gives your skin its colour. Freckles and moles are formed where there is a high concentration of melanin. People aren't born with freckles. They develop in the top layer of skin during childhood and in later years as a result of repeated sun exposure. A mole is a small cluster of melanocytes in the second layer of skin and it is usually present soon after birth.

Why does our hair turn grey when we get old?

Each hair on our head is made up of a shaft – the coloured part we can see – and a root, which attaches the hair to our scalp. Under the skin the root is surrounded by a hair follicle, which contains pigment cells that continuously produce a chemical called melanin. Melanin gives hair its colour of brown, blonde, red and anything in between and is the same stuff that makes our skin fair or dark. Hair goes grey because as we get older, pigment cells stop producing melanin. Without melanin, our hair becomes a more transparent colour – such as grey, silver or white.

mela-who?

wart are you looking at?

aff tha
doesn't
nething
d closes
ry scab-m
y, OOZin
ssness. Can t
-green, browny
ons.

You can develop warts just like you can catch a cold. It's a virus that, like other germs, hangs around waiting for an unsuspecting kid to pick it up. The virus that causes warts is called the human papilloma virus or HPV for short. The wart virus is passed from person to person and loves warm, moist places like small cuts or scratches on your hands or feet, which is why you're more likely to catch it if you bite your nails. But don't worry, most warts are benign, which means they won't harm you.

Why do old people have wrinkles?

The skin has three layers: the epidermis, the dermis and the subcutaneous layer. All three work together to keep the skin in tip-top shape. When you're young, the skin does a great job of stretching and holding in moisture. But over time, the dermis loses both collagen and elastin. The skin gets thinner and has trouble getting moisture to the epidermis. The fat in the subcutaneous layer that gives skin a plump appearance also begins to disappear and the epidermis starts to sag – and you wrinkle!

Why is the chicken pox called chicken pox?

The 'chicken' part of chicken pox comes from the Latin word 'cicer', which means 'chick pea'. Apparently, back when people were sitting around thinking up names for diseases, they thought chicken pox blisters looked like chickpeas. Which, in a way, they do. Chickpeas are round, yellowish, bean-like vegetables, which you usually eat in salads! 'Cicer' is pronounced 'cheeker', which somehow became chicken over time. The result: a bunch of people wondering if you can get chicken pox from chickens – which you can't!

Why do pimples have pus?

Pus is an important part of your body's defence against infection. It is made up of a special kind of white blood cell called neutrophils. Their main job is to eat and digest invading micro-organisms such as bacteria – and pimples are full of bacteria! Bacteria eat and poop and eat and poop and make a real mess. White blood cells arrive to clean up the mess. In the process of fighting off infection, they die. So pus is a battleground full of soldiers, living and dead.

Why do people get ingrown toenails?

If you trim your toenails too short or cut them curved, get ready for an ingrown toenail. Why? Because cutting your nail like this encourages it to grow into the skin of your toe. The sides of the nail curl down and dig into your skin. Wearing shoes that are too tight or too short can also cause an ingrown toenail. And they're nasty! First the skin around the nail gets hard, swollen and tender, then red, infected and sore. Finally, your skin may start to grow over the ingrown toenail. So be safe and cut straight.

Skin - the stuff t'
making sure your b
no flavour.
   Scabs - so
hat appears when
Sometimes eaten v
munchers.
Pus - A runny,
...rry of grossn
...een, brown, yell...

What is tinea?

Tinea, or athlete's foot, is a skin infection caused by fungus, a plant-like micro-organism that loves to get into areas of your body where it's warm and moist. Once it finds a nice warm spot on your skin it moves in and starts growing and spreading. To grow, the fungus needs dead tissue for nutrition. And there's plenty of that on your feet! Although anyone, not just athletes, can get tinea, it is easily managed with treatments available in chemists.

Does your hair still grow after you are dead?

Hair doesn't continue to grow after you die; it's all optical illusion. Dead is dead. The only things growing after you're dead are worms, bacteria, and other parasites. What is happening, however, is that the skin around the hair dehydrates and shrinks. Our flesh dries and in doing so doing pulls away from the hair, making it look longer, as if it had grown.

Why do we get lice?

Head lice are excellent crawlers! And if for some reason your hair touches someone else's (who has lice) you could get lice too. Lice can also be spread through sharing things such as hats, towels, helmets, hair ties and so on. Usually there are only about 12 active lice on a head at one time, but it's the eggs that are the problem! The female louse produces an extremely strong glue-like substance that attaches the egg to the hair, which makes it very hard to get rid of them. She lays at a rate of about six eggs each night. The eggs hatch and are ready to lay eggs themselves within five days. So getting rid of them sooner is better than later.

itch itch itch itch

Skin - t
making su
lavour.
Scabs - so
when a wound
when picked by hungry scab-munchers.
Pus – A runny, oozing, gloopy, liquid
slurry of grossness. Can be white, yellow,

Blood & Body Bits

What makes blood clot?

Although a healthy person can lose as much as one-third of their blood and still live, the body doesn't handle it very well and that's why we have platelets. Platelets are tiny, irregularly shaped, colourless bodies that travel in our blood. When our skin is broken, they stick to each other to try and stop the blood coming out. They also release a chemical that causes your blood to make fibres called fibrin. These are just like a net that traps the blood cells. If the cut is small, you'll soon have a clot. Where the clot is exposed to the air, a scab forms. Meanwhile your body starts repairing the damage. So although scabs may look ugly – don't pick them, they are there for a reason!

Why are veins blue?

Light is made up of many different colours, which are absorbed at different rates by your skin. A vein looks blue because red light travels far enough into the skin to be absorbed by the blood in the vein. Blue light can't travel this far and is reflected back through your skin. Also – veins pump blood back to the heart. This blood has no oxygen, and without oxygen, blood loses some of its colour. It looks darker and purplish – even blue.

have I eaten too many blueberries?

What is the brain made of?

Just because the brain looks like a soft, pink-grey, over-sized walnut doesn't mean it's gross. Your brain tissue floats in cerebrospinal fluid, which cushions it from damaging knocks. The tissue is made up of about 100 million nerve cells called neurons. These send electrical signals to each other in a massive network. This network does everything from controlling your breathing, to storing information and thinking. Yet although the brain is a very amazing organ, we still know very little about it.

What are ticks and how do they get on animals?

Ticks are bloodsucking parasites that feed on humans and animals. A tick's guts and skin are designed to expand as it ingests blood. There are over 850 tick species, 100 of which can transmit diseases. Ticks are arachnids, like mites and spiders. Ticks don't fly, jump, or blow around with the wind; they simply wait patiently for a host. Their sensory organs are complex and can detect gases such as carbon dioxide produced by warm-blooded animals from far away.

EEP!

KRAK!

oints produce that CRACK when bubbles burst in the fluid surrounding the joint. Joints in the fingers are composed of two bones, held together by a strong, fibrous capsule and ligaments. A thick, clear lubricant (made mostly of carbon dioxide and some nitrogen) called synovial fluid is found between these bones. When you stretch or pull your finger, the bones pull apart and pressure is reduced on the synovial fluid. This allows the gas to form bubbles that quickly expand and then burst causing that 'popping' sound.

orn with it and are
ould look after it. Unless you are an
ANDROID or ROBOT.

Not all worms can live if you cut them in half, but the earthworms that you're probably familiar with can! They have amazing healing powers to help them survive. If you cut a worm in half, both sides will continue wiggling. If the cut is after the segments that contains vital organs the portion with the head may grow a new tail! The tail portion will just continue to wiggle until the nerve cells die. But how cool is this! Some worms have a natural reflex, by which they will eject their tail when the tail is pulled. Perfect for escaping birds looking for a tasty worm lunch!

How were leeches used in medicine?

Hah hah hah! You thought leeches were only used in the olden days, didn't you! Well they were but they're also used today! A leech's saliva contains chemicals that numb pain and stop blood from clotting so your blood will flow freely when you're bitten. In the 1800s, doctors were fond of 'bloodletting' and used leeches all the time. These days leeches are used after surgery to regain circulation in re-attached body parts.

Why do chickens eat their own eggs when they are broken?

If an egg breaks, most chickens can't resist eating it, partly because they're trying to make up for whatever nutrients they aren't getting in their feed. The yolk is full of nutrients and the shell gives them the calcium and protein they need to make more eggshells. But it might also be that the hens simply like the taste. If chickens are breaking eggs to eat them and you want to discourage them, then try filling an egg with something that tastes gross or spicy!

eggcellent!!

Vile Breath

& Belching

ad Breath

Breath is found wafting from
ch when they speak to you o
unfortunate SMOOCHER
inds of Bad Breath – all are re
D, here's just a few:

RENT Breath – When you eat
wn-uppish stuff like oysters
argot (snails) and garli

art Breath – Breath
outh that could be mist
ming from one's butt. G om
ints if this is you.

odzilla Breath – VERY BA ng
reath.
Radi The kind th
hat i
and s
botto

Why does soft drink make you burp?

A burp is nothing more than gas escaping
from your stomach. When you eat, drink and
breathe, you swallow air, which is full of gases
such as nitrogen and oxygen. Any extra gas in
your stomach is forced up and out of your mouth ...
burp! When you drink soft drink you might find that
you burp more. Why? Because these drinks contain
carbon dioxide to make them fizzy. Carbon dioxide
is a gas that needs to get out! If the gas is trapped
in your large intestine, it comes out the other end
– oops!

Why do we get bad breath?

Garlic and onions are famous for causing our breath to smell anything but sweet, but they're not the only culprits. Bacteria in our mouths, which feast on left-over bits of food and let off very smelly sulfur compounds, cause bad breath. The medical name for it is halitosis and you can also get it from gum disease and sinus problems. But maybe what you don't realise is, there's another area in the mouth that carries the odour of bad breath – your tongue. So make sure you remember to brush it!

Crusty Eyes

During the day, tears keep your eyes clean and moist; at night tear fluid isn't needed because your eyes are closed and protected. However, without a fresh supply of liquid, tears that are left on the surface of your eye can't drain as easily into the tear ducts below your eyes. So all night long, a goopy mix of sweat, oils, protein and fat from your tears seep out and collect near the caruncle (that's the fleshy bump) in the corner of your eye. And by morning you have yourself a nice dried-up crust!

Eye Crust EYE ...
...ke a kind of ...
...lty flavour, s...
...pposed to be...
...ich is quit...
...nk about

How do we get conjunctivitis?

Y ou rub your eyes, but they won't stop itching ... when you look in the mirror, they're red, puffy and rimmed with yellowish eye-gunk. What's going on? You have a very common eye problem – conjunctivitis! Most people get it from bacteria or viruses, but it can also be caused by allergies. Some bacteria and viruses cause the protective membrane covering your eye, called the conjunctiva, to swell up. This leads to itchiness, redness and swelling. You get this form of conjunctivitis, which is very contagious, by rubbing your eyes with hands that have come into contact with the germs! Remember, germs are microscopic so you won't be able to see them – so washing your hands regularly helps prevent this! However, if the conjunctivitis is caused by allergens it's not catchy.

How do people get blood-shot eyes?

If you look very closely in the mirror, you'll see that the whites of your eyes contain thousands of tiny blood vessels. Normally, they're so small that they don't discolour the eye's white areas, but when things such as dust, pollen, dry air or sun annoy our eyes, the vessels become puffed up with blood and the eyes look red. When an area becomes irritated, extra blood flows to the problem area and releases chemicals that help in the healing process. So although it may look gruesome, it's just a sign that your body's healing itself.

What's inside your eyeballs?

Lots! And all those gross bits (even all those bright-red blood vessels) play a very important role. The eyeball, like a camera, needs a lens to focus light and a film (or the retina) on which to focus the rays. The retina captures the image and sends it to the brain to be developed. The iris (coloured part) opens and closes to let more or less light into the eye through to the pupil (the black bit). The sclera (white part) has the job of protecting everything inside. And it's those yucky-looking blood vessels that nourish the outer layers of the retina.

Why do onions make people cry?

Like other plants, onions are made of cells. These cells are divided into two sections separated by a membrane. One side has a chemical called an enzyme; the other side has molecules that contain sulfur. When you slice an onion, the contents on each side mix together – and that's when it starts to sting. Chemical reactions take place and gas is formed. It reacts with the water in your eyes and produces sulfuric acid. Ouch! Your eyes produce tears because your body wants to wash or dilute the chemicals that irritate your eyes.

Is it true that if you hold your eyes open while you sneeze they can pop out?

When you sneeze, water droplets fly out of your mouth at an explosive 120 kilometres per hour! So you could think that if you keep your eyes open, they might pop out. But they won't! Our eyes are very secure in their sockets. They snap shut by reflex, which gives the impression that your body is doing its best to keep your eyes firmly in place.

1. Eye Crust EYE POO!
Like a kind of
Salty flavour, sandy colour.
Supposed to be left there by Fairy's,
which is quite rude when you

Why do flies have so many eyes?

Flies don't have many eyes – what they have is many lenses. Flies can have 4000 lenses in each eye! Adult insects have two compound eyes and up to three simple eyes on the tops of their heads. Each compound eye consists of many single eyes, which are independent from each other. Each lens catches its own image. The two large eyes of a fly give an almost complete 360-degree vision. But compound eyes can't be focussed, so flies see everything in a blurred image. However, compound eyes see things very quickly. Flies can immediately detect even the slightest movement – like a fly swatter coming.

Stinky Pits

Why does sweat smell?

We sweat to cool down. Now sweat itself doesn't make that bad smell, it's the tiny bacteria munching on it that does it. When you become a teenager, the sweat under your arms becomes thicker and smells a bit (in a good way). You see, the sweat now gives off special smells called pheromones (fer-oh-moans). These are smells that attract animals to each other. They are also found in perfumes. The problem is, bacteria love this new sweat under your arms, so they munch away. Soon your underarms start smelling, which is why teenagers and grown-ups use deodorant – kids don't need to.

1. St
The s
stand
prom
smel
by s
(als

Why do pigs roll in mud?

Maybe because they like it ... it keeps them cool, stops them getting sunburnt and helps rid their bodies of parasites such as fleas and lice. We humans sweat to cool down. As the moisture on us evaporates, it takes our heat away. But pigs, like dogs and cats, can't sweat. So pigs will roll in whatever wet thing – like mud – is handy, to cool down. The moisture on them works the same way as our sweat does.

Stinky Pit
the smell is often
stands for Bod
ounced BEE-
y person's a
weat and con
called BC

Pits
often called
ody Ou
BEE-OH, wafts
n's armpits
combated with
BO-masher

Why do people grow hairs under their arms?

Our bodies change from the day we're born until the day we die. The brain knows when the body is nearing maturity and releases chemicals called hormones that are responsible for different changes. One of the first signs of puberty is hair growth. Perhaps one reason we grow underarm hair is to help us cool down when we sweat. Sweating is the body's major way of getting rid of excess body heat and keeping us cool.

WARNING WARNI
may off
may offend!

Festy Feet

toast anyone?

What is toejam?

That icky stuff between your toes comes from bacteria dining on the fatty acids in the sweat that pours out of the foot's pores. It gets jammed there and mixes with sock fabric, sweat and dirt as a result of you wearing shoes and socks. But it's not only dead bacteria that give that gunk between your toes a bad odour; it's also their piles of waste – ewww!

Brain Freeze

Don't blame the ice-cream. Blame the roof of your mouth, your nerves and your blood vessels. Here's the scoop... When something very cold touches the centre of the roof of your mouth, the nerves overreact to the cold temperature and try to heat up your brain. The nerves cause the blood vessels in your brain to swell up. And it's that quick swelling that causes your head to pound and hurt – not freeze!

Earwax

Why do people have wax in their ears?

Your ear makes wax to repel water, trap dust, fight germs and even catch small bugs. You shouldn't put anything in your ears to clean the wax out because you might just push more wax in and plug up your ear. Old earwax falls out in tiny dry clumps all the time – which means you're leaving a trail of earwax behind you right now!

Is it true that giraffes use their tongues to clean out their ears?

Yes! Giraffes' tongues can be over 0.5m long. Their tongues are so long they can wrap them entirely around the head. They're also useful for cleaning out ears. The only thing we haven't worked out is whether they do it because they like clean ears or because their earwax just tastes so yummy – maybe it's both!

Yellow Teeth

Plaque is a thin, sticky, colourless bacteria that forms on your teeth. And if you don't give your teeth a good brush regularly it turns into hardened, yellow tartar – ewww. Teeth are actually made up of several layers. The middle layer, the dentine, is the thickest layer and is yellow in colour. The visible layer is the white enamel and is only a narrow strip. Plaque sticks to the teeth and makes acids that slowly eat away at the protective enamel surface of the teeth, which makes holes. Teeth always look a little yellow because of the reflection of the yellow dentine seeping through.

Belly Button Fluff

& Dandruff

Where does belly button fluff come from?

Funnily enough, 'Ignoble Prize' winner Dr Karl Kruszelnicki has just finished a survey of 4799 people regarding this. It seems belly button fluff mainly comes from clothes fibres, although no-one knows for certain what it's made from. We're more likely to get fluff if our belly button is an 'innie' rather than an 'outtie' (makes sense) and – don't gross out on this one – if we have a trail of hair leading to our belly button.

What is dandruff made of?

Dandruff is made up of dead skin cells, oil and sometimes dirt. Millions of skin cells are shed every day from all over your body, even from your scalp. You also have oil-making glands at the base of the hair follicles on your scalp. Sometimes these glands get aggravated and make too much oil. This can cause the skin flakes to clump together to form white flakes or 'dandruff'. Everyone has dandruff to some degree. It can be aggravated by not washing enough or washing too much, by stress or by infections. But the main thing to know is that it is not contagious.

Pins'n'Needles

Why do we
get pins
and needles?

Nerves are like tiny threads or wires that run through your whole body and carry messages back and forth between your brain and body. If you sit in a funny position or the same position for a long time, the nerves sometimes get squeezed and the signals can't get through properly, and that's when you can't feel anything! As they begin to stretch back to their regular shape and send signals again, that's when you feel that strange pins-and-needles sensation.

Mould

Mould starts life as tiny little spores. These spores are present all around us in the air. If a spore lands on your food then it will start to grow and soon your food will be covered in that icky green stuff. Mould needs air to live and prefers warm, dark places. As every school kid knows, the perfect conditions for growing mould exist in the school bag, where many a sandwich has met an untimely – and mouldy – death.

Thank you to all these So Gross fans for their awesome So Gross questions!

Aaron Collins
Alan Massie
Alana Giaquinta
Alyssa Douglas
Angus Watkins
Anita Ilier
Anna Fetterplace
April Prime

Ariana Bautovich
Ayden Browne
Bedia Kisa
Ben Robinson
Ben Smith
Bianca Berto
Blade Hooper
Breanna Shields

Bre-Anne Sandercock
Carly Giddler
Celia Gercovich
Chris Chandler
Damon Gear
Deanne Toomer
Eli Wilinski
Ellena Walls

Ellie-Jane Rix
Elliott Williams
Emily Nelson
Emma Schultz
Fern Siebler
Frances Lindsay
Harry Pagliaro
Helen Alexander

Irina Chitez
Jackson Gunther
James Bell
Jamie Henderson
Jemima Buckman
Jenna
Jess Smith
Jesse Bayer

Joel Steller
John Tonbi-Filippini
Jordan Fleming
Jordan Johnson
Jordan Scott
Josh Talbot
Joshua Brown
Katie O'Brien

Kimberley Lipszye
Kyle Newton
Lang Teh
Lauren Alexander
Leonard Price
Liam Hodges
Lilian Zhu
Louise Craker

Makayla Rimmington
Manon Edwards
Matt Holt
Matt Layland
Matthew Parsons
Matthew Pluckrose
Matthew Stone
Michael Fullwood

Michael Siers
Mikaela Parker
Mitchell Williams
Monique Siebenhausen
Naomi Hoarsely
Natalie S
Nicholas Brown
Nicole Maclean

Oliver Galke
Petal Green
Rafael Gonzalez
Rania Abed
Rebecca Pennell
Renae Green
Ron Swarzmann
Rudan
Sam Cottle

Sam Poplawski
Sarah Siebenhausen
Sidney Shen
Stephanie Zhu
Taylor Johnson
Timandra Christiansen
Timothy White
Timothy Robson
Timothy Trewern

Tom Simpson
Trent Gray
Trent Petronaitis
Troy Fernance
Vytus Jarasius
Wayne Turner
Will Sandry
Willem Brussen
Zack Henshaw